Tongue in Ink

ISBN: 979-821-86558-4-6

Library of Congress Control Number 2025906986

Poetry by Shannon P. Laws
Artwork by Kathleen A. McKeever
Book design by Jill Flores

Published in association with
Village Books and Paper Dreams
1200 11th Street
Bellingham, WA 98225
villagebooks.com

Printed in the United States of America by IngramSpark

SHANNON LAWS

Tongue in Ink

VILLAGE BOOKS
AND
PAPER DREAMS
BUILDING COMMUNITY SINCE 1980

Dedication

To my family.

I am indebted to the Corridor Collective, which supports the *Corridor* zine project. This book gives a wink to the zine. It is a remarkable experiment started in 2022 that explores the connection between found art and synchronicities.

"Shannon Laws paints ephemeral moments, transporting the reader to these glimpses of nature and existence. Thoughts of love, meditations on silence, and brief moments of peace. It's a wonderful series of miniature vacations to better places."

— **Duncan Shields**, author of *Small Windows*

"From a bed of messy covers to a stroll along Whatcom Creek, Shannon Laws' *Tongue in Ink* immerses us in intimate and familiar spaces. Impermanence unites the collection, making Kathleen McKeever's intriguing collages an inspired choice for the book's illustrations. There is light, love, pain, gentle humor and so much generous humanity within these pages. *Tongue in Ink* is a gift from a treasured and spectacularly talented Bellingham poet."

— **Mary Vermillion**, community relations manager,
Whatcom County Library System

"In *Tongue in Ink*, Shannon Laws shares poems of everyday magic, as she celebrates both the thrill and ache of living and loving. They are presented in warm organic tones, grounded in sensual detail … and then, every so often, you get hit with a zinger—an image, a turn of phrase, a whole poem--that turns the world upside down."

— **Kevin Murphy**, author of *The Last Normal Year*

Tongue in Ink, offers a collection of image-rich poems and thought-provoking collages. Visually compelling and emotionally open, Laws' poems explore themes of love and loss, and the nature of change: "a past covered over and over with false stories of a forgotten past." The poems in *Tongue in Ink* question the nature of relationships, the seasons, spirits, and time being a riddle we'll never understand. *Tongue in Ink* is a beautiful volume of poetry.

— **Nancy Canyon**, author of *Struck* (memoir) and *Saltwater* (poetry)

Tongue in Ink is a compilation of old and new work that offers insight, delight, and variety. Readers get amusing observation … as well as gritty candor. I found choice lines in "Almost 8" in which Laws describes people going to work: the professionals "those bleached-sterile by fluorescent, preserved in recycled air" and the typical backpack-wearing, biking 'Hamster who "navigates through the intersection Railroad & Chestnut, the traffic light only a suggestion." Artist Kathleen A. McKeever's "watch-centered" collage is a perfect accompaniment, as are all two dozen of her creations.

— **Linda Quinby Lambert**, writer and
2024 Village Books Literary Citizenship Award recipient

In *Tongue in Ink*, Shannon Laws exposes what is extraordinary about the everyday. With senses attuned to details borne of the rhythms of life, Laws invites you into the domestic realm where the scent of onions mingles with the rustle of newspaper, where "calloused hands turn inky pages," and where stories unfold in the quiet corners of home. Even the second-hand mattress tells a story of the inescapably familiar, "First night—I rolled into a dip / A body-shaped dip." In this collection where kisses become temporary tattoos and history is molded into fingers, poems are unabashedly visceral, taking on the body, the living and the dying. Ultimately, *Tongue in Ink* speaks to the human condition, reflecting an awareness of both the limitations of a life and the joy of living it.

— **Maria McLeod**, author of *Skin. Hair. Bones.*

Table of Contents

"We are volcanoes. When we women offer our
experience as our truth, as human truth,
all the maps change. There are new mountains."

—Ursula K. Le Guin

Saturday's Song

Sunny Saturday
Beams filter through
The sheer curtained window
Onto the stage of us;
A bed of messy covers

Softly, gently
You sing and strum
I lie next to you and listen
Watching your fingers move

Our song of love
Fills the room
Our hearts
Our minds
Mix in the melody

Your fingers travel down
The chords of my spine.
Play me, love me
Like you loved that song

...and you do

River Ink

Went to the river looking for a poem
I found my familiar trail
winding woods that hug the bank

Whatcom Creek in August:
bushes high and
full of berries,
birds and spider's webs

Grass sways underwater
moving in sync with the river
This is what peace looks like
melted into movement

Tree branch dips over the drink
desiring more of plenty
is water from the root not good enough
or do you cool your leaves in the noon sun

Down by the edge, two dead trees have
slumped across making a place to sit

I dip a stick into the stream
like pen into ink
to write my name on
the sun-bleached wood

The sun grabs my letters
throws them in the air
birds ride the upward current
Did I just disappear?

Tempest

This morning the sky changed.
Wind from another direction casts surprise
and stirred up curiosity

Trees above sway to the song of fall,
make for a lovely dance to sing to
Below, wind combs through underbrush,
grabs the recently fallen,
blows them into whirlwinds

Northern Gale, breathe on me,
release from me dead and dying parts
Twirl them up to the sky, lay them on the ground
Churn them into soil; all that death is good for
Compost for a garden I have yet to harvest

Wink

Morning sunlight, sun low
stretch shadows long
twinkle through the branches
that sway in the current
bathe me please

Stronger the light
Harsher the dark

Sun cannot be everywhere
nature's landscape prevents it
God made or not

Crow flies by
nods its head
as if it remembers me

Your life so simple Crow
Please brood over my features
A wink when you fly by will let me know
They are fixed in your mind

The Sun may not always find me
Yet your wings move you
amongst the penumbras

Your nod, Crow, brings me comfort
for somewhere, by someone
I am remembered

Monday Night And
I Missed The Last Bus

Sure stepping down the long south slope behind the college
pitch black out, the on-coming cars blind me, for a long
second the sidewalk disappears, each car tests me.
Walking by faith I believe the ground is still there.
Sideways rain covers my glasses.

At a crossing, I'm touched by the beauty of a street lamp
standing guard, burning amber on everything directly below:
the street, a bush, a hedge, an ornamental
cherry tree drooping heavy

I grab my phone to take a photo
as soon as it touches the wet air, it dies.
Now I am an island.
Walking through the sleeping suburbs
nose pointed home.

Last Hour of the Night

Night traffic flows in irregular patterns
Swoosh by in shades of shadow and streetlight
Some tires find the manhole cover
Bounce off it adding tenor to the jazz

Drops of 4 a.m. dew touch down
On grass tips torching each blade
The lawn is now a million moons
Silently lit with the white of diamonds
Slugs ride the water highway
Fast path to someone's petunias
As a raccoon wiggles low, out of the brush
Carpet-cleaning body wets her underbelly

Too late for conversation
Too early for work
The world paints a peaceful moment
So real, I stand in it

Her Hands

The door squeaks hello as I enter her sanctuary
The leather garden glove still holds the hand
I see it
It is the first thing I see

History molded into each finger strip
crooked right pointer finger
bump on the left where a ring sat
blacken ends that dipped in fresh soil
over and over

The pair rests near a dirt encrusted terra cotta pot,
shears in a sleeve, the handle still shining.
Hedge trimmer hangs on a bent brown nail
frozen, half open

But, the bulbs,
the bulbs below the counter
hidden in a beat up cardboard box
the to-be-planted promises
carry the weight of the room

She was ready for the early spring.

Grasp

Mist disappears into clean air
Turns into the space between us

We once were something no one could hold
All could see, none will breathe

It was an occurrence that clings under limbs
a pairing like lady slipper and pine

Grasp at straws that floss between fingers
Reach for yesterday's fog

Winter Sunset

Sun setting at three pm
getting ready for bed
shade is drawn on
the west window
Conversations bounce
off hard wood
spoons clink in
white bowls
Does the sun
hear my pen
scrape across the page
Can the woman
with red hair
hear the bubbles
sparkle in my cup

September Bellingham

Down the hill my city sits
Waves nip at it's hair
Freeway scratches the belly
Mountains hold down it's hip
Low mist rolled in early
refuses to leave this cove
Down into the clouds I walk
floating up into a subdued world
Here exhales are marked
Talk can be seen
Sun bathes buildings
in a peach-warm glow
as it fights the floating moisture
that crowns my
September Bellingham.
Noon-thirty,
visibility still
only four blocks
The sun burns
while seagulls
dance in the sky

Almost 8

Morning beer bottles gather on the last
step laid over, laid up, slept past last call
My coffee in too small a cup sits
with me at a table that limps

Construction worker walks from sandwich shop to truck,
early enough for the dirty professions, still too
early for the clean, those bleached-sterile
by fluorescent, preserved in recycled air

Trash in the bushes, empty cup rolls
along in this morning wind
will it be enough to push over clouds
that fill this window

There's my man! A 'Hamster: suit and soft shoe, on his bike,
backpack full of papers, phone, protein bar, water
He navigates through the intersection of Railroad & Chestnut,
the traffic light only a suggestion

* A "Hamster" is an endearing name for a citizen of Bellingham

Dry Unwanted Parts

There is a pile
back by the fence
winters clippings cross stacked
It waits.
     It waits–
for gas
for the snap of a match
The sky to scroll back
the dead to rise
the heavy unable to move
the thin blown like leaves

Leaf Tattoo

You can you feel it
In my city
The change of air
as wind folds in
fall's weather.

Orange leaves appear on
the sidewalks of Holly Street.
No worms to dance them back to soil.

Cement laden, laid on
the roadside in random patterns
leave a tattoo, imprinted on the stone.
Five pointed star tree hand
pressed by feet and rain
bleed orange ink for all to see.

By winter the marks wash away
By spring, bright green babies wave
at us from their mother's arm borne
back into our memory.

Ink Stained Hands

Read me the paper Uncle
Loud enough to hear in the kitchen
Touch it for me, turn those pages
Aunties and I are cooking dinner
hands must be kept clean
But in your place by the fire
the beige recliner squeaks
on the back-beat of your rocking
Toes slide in and out of leather
slippers stretched out and soft
as a first basemen's glove
Calloused hands turn each inky
page of the Sunday review
Headlines shout at us
while we chop onions

Death's Dip
or Confession of a Mattress

FREE mattress. A queen size pillow top
Took it home, laid it in the frame
First night—I rolled into a dip
a body shaped dip
on the left side

A person taller than me, wider than me
created a dip that I roll into
a bedridden, sickly person
left a death dip

No problem, I think, I'll just sleep on the right
every night to even things out
Yet, every morning I wake in the dip

My bed, now a metaphorical display
divides my psyche down the middle
The dip is comfortable, soft, form fitting
It feels like a hug in my lonely bed.

It is as comfortable as my father's depression,
a heavy-known feeling of failure,
like a person reluctant to leave their bed
My familiar spin tires set on park.

This I confess to you:
I sleep with death
—and I like it

Skin Suit Sewn Too Tightly

As a doctor sucks poison from a bite
the red rock of Bisbee calls out ghosts
The dead come back to walk again
Reincarnation of secondhand spirits
as secondhand furniture

The dresser is painted now
The couch new cloth
The set of chairs split apart
The headboard used for vines

the painting under the painting
a past covered over and over
with false stories of forgotten moments

Moments made to fill the gap of time
the hungry use between reading
the menu—ordering the meal

Fat of the present melts off
dead blood returns moisture to the air
dries your muscles tight

Tight as new couch fabric
White as the dresser
Your set of ribs pull apart
Your head a plot of vines

Wrong Seat

Chair with no backing
Broken spring somewhere
Its cushion a questionable color Pattern selected or an historic stain? Must
test if still wet

> *Sit here if you like*
> *It's the last chair left*
> *And it is just not right*

Your frame will not fit
The Seuss-wobbled structure Yet you sit. It is the last chair. Bottom line
discovers the
Displeasure immediately

Work Boots

At the end of the night
the mill is put to bed
engineers walk the plant
lock the doors
leave the lights on
in the lead-red firerooms

My boots rest
on the home stoop
of a feathered nest
built for one

I sleep hard
wake a day later
wanting the world
to be different

It is not

Monday arrives
with a wink
my boots
ready to absorb more
soggy disappointment

The Riddle

I am a net
tossed into the sea.
Weights in the corner
drag me down.
     One hard jerk
     secures the catch.
     Winch and pulley
     draw me back.
Wet and heavy with
dinner and debris
If I could be used
for something different
     Tablecloth
     Rug
     Curtains
A net to hold fruit,
a wall hanging,
broken apart, unraveled,
re-knitted into a sweater.

But I am a fishnet
thrown to the storm
My value—
caught between spaces.

35

Crab

Foam washed wreckage to shore
breath-bubbles pop in the thin light

Early beachcomber fights the gulls
for a freshly delivered treasure

The minute before dawn you grab its back
Carry it to your kitchen for a slow boil

With a crack, a glut of juices spills out
Lips suck at the muscle and warm butter

An ear to the empty skin hears echoes of the sea
Drink your drink, sit in your chair, look out the window
and stare—
She was a good wife. It was a good life.

No New Day

The days return
familiar moments
eyelashes point at a paper
no words can dance on
flower faces open
peeks inside the window
fingers weave the story of us
a braided rug used to
cover the blemish

On my shoulder you perch
squawk as a chore,
as a word to cross off

Your kiss, a temporary tattoo
placed on my flesh with spit

Thailand Rug

Take off your dungaree jacket
come and sit by the high fire
warm yourself for brisket
dry 'yer socks for tomorra'

You are a sailor, not a farm to toil
around the globe, you float on your mistress Sea
let saltwater then heal your gashes
You'll only get good soil from me

My blood is full of vinegar
shake it on top 'yer cod
fork a big bite for your mouth to light
then perhaps you'll meet your god

Truly the Lord lives in the fish,
fillet batter and flake-white
Rest your head on my bosom port
Tie a tail to your colorful kite

Let's rip the sheets up tonight, love
then move onto the floor
to cut up the Thailand rug, dear
that's really from Singapore

Oh rest your head on top my bosom port
tie your boat to my nested lap
tell those ladies on faraway shores
you're in love, dear, and won't be back

Triple Hit

There was a man named Ned
who liked his ladies three
thrice was the number he bed
triple the pleasure to bounce on his knee

Only one at a time did he enjoy
the curves of each lovely lady
His best trickery he did employ
none suspected Ned as shady

One lady as thin as a finger
another voluptuous as melons
the third a passion fruit that lingers
He dined on each like a felon

One day all three arrived at the same spot!
Thrice were face-slaps spent on Ned!
Triple was the number he was shot!
On the stone that lays at his head—

Here lies Ned lover of three
Brought down by a 22-caliber
While in midst of a loving spree
Forgot to update his calendar

Fire Works

An empty envelope
Never licked
I wrote your name three times
Folded the paper twice
Added to the
Backyard burning barrel
A cauldron full of
Last week's newspaper
Fall leaves
And a folded letter
With your name on it
Pages of my diary
An old photo of me
taken without permission
Burn. Burn. Burn.
Done.

Christopher Titus Save Me

"...our bodies were worn, our spirits whipped. there was a sense of unreality." —the 12-hour night by Charles Bukowski

I found myself in middle age working the graveyard shift as a deep cleaner at a casino, and somehow there seemed to be no way out

I was smothered by
waist-less women
in high heels
butts in the ashtrays
butts in the seats
baseball hats on empty heads
guts spilling over large buckles
Work boots and flip-flops
bring an endless
amount of pine needles
and waffle-mud cakes
Everything looks too tight
especially the Tuesday Tweakers

I am drained here
my life is ending
but, Christopher Titus is coming
—in February

He smiles at me from the poster's place on each side
of each four-sided pillar and near the door
"As seen on Comedy Central"
"Get your tickets now"
Christopher is coming!
His spiky blonde hair and blue eyes hold life

He is my savior in an ash-covered world
As I sweep up pieces of paper, fingernails, toothpicks,
squeezed-out limes from the casino's clown colored floor

I imagine sweet Christopher busting through the main
entrance on a
white steed
shining
he is shining

glowing with a bright future
a future he offers me if only
I wash off my Cinderella ashes
take his hand and leave this place
Oh, how he glows

He talks to me—
Why are you here? C'mon, you can do better
You're wiping up blood and vomit from slot machines.
Your new "skill" is how to reach into the bathroom garbage
to avoid a hidden syringe, -and the SHRIMP on Friday Fish Day!
All that half-chewed shrimp clogging up your vacuum!
C'mon!
look at ME
look how happy I am
join me in this happiness

I was so tired, so dazed, my anguish mixed with hopelessness
I saw myself fifteen years from now, hunched over the sweeper
being called darlin' and sugar, taking empty glasses once full
of spirits, offering clean ashtrays
I talked sense to my Titan
This isn't so bad
I've learned much more than biohazard clean up
I've studied this species of human
that gamble

You can learn a lot from the way they put out their cigarettes
Like footprints in the snow, you know what animal has walked by
 The Texan—punches the butt straight down; it stands erect
 The Cowboy— rolled and smashed, falls to the side
 The Camper—sits at the same machine for hours, same butt brand
 overfills the ashtray
 The Britney— pink lipstick on the butt, usually a camper
 Ladybird— smokes the very thin lady cigarette, flutters around
 from machine to machine
Still, my Titan smiles

Then one night I stood up for myself and left
My last day is this Friday, I told my shift manager on Thursday
You found something else
Yes
Yes, I did
fresh air and dignity
It pays nothing

On my last day, I handed in my badge
I returned my uniforms
left my locker unlocked
Christopher Titus had come and gone
A new act was plastered on the pillars
I turned and walked away
into the night
and my life was
touched by magic
and it
still
is

45

Housekeeper

People of all types
Come and go to my hotel
The same room will house
Many different lives

Some stay for less than eight hours
Others for days
Each time I reset the room
Removing the evidence of a life

I know them now when they walk in
Not by name or by hometown
I know them by their stains
The marks left behind, that I clean

For you, I'll find wine rings
Dried on the tables
Some spills on the sheets
Bottles in the garbage

For you, I'll find diapers
Filling both waste baskets
Spit-up on the bed cover
A travel crib I'll have to take down

For you, I'll find almost nothing
You made your bed before leaving
Your shower was too quick to dirty
Changing the sheets, I'll find a sock

I clean the room
The same room
Over and over
I clean you away

Washing the tub
Scrubbing off the ring
Removing the hair
Wiping down the mirror

Dusting the room
Making the bed
Vacuuming it all away
You are gone

Honey Jar

He still calls me honey
That jar is long empty
A few amber crystals
Cling to the inside

      How long until the pet names stop
      'til a new sweetener is found

Perhaps a Sweet n' Low will find him
Maybe an Equal will catch his eye
He'll bless the day high fructose corn syrup
Tap dances into his heart

Honey he may call it
But honey it will never be
His appetite for sweets
Sends him on a consuming safari
Like a lion roaring in the streets

      All are given a portion of true love
      How quickly he consumes his
      Cursing the empty jar
      Redirecting the blame

Artificial sweeteners only bring to mind
Memories you can't return to
Hunger pains for what cannot spoil
Honey kisses that always satisfied

49

South Beach

Often, we would walk South Beach together
That long large-pebbled beach
along the Salish Sea
on the island's west side

    Short, saltwater waves
    lap up against the shore there,
    constant rhythm set by the wind,
    like a slow rock tumbler
    sifting for agates

Brown cliffs of San Juan
barely hold a road on top itself
Large crumbles of dirt clots
lay at its feet predicting its fate

Hard soles are needed to walk this beach
The stones just large enough to
aggravate the arches as you walk,
Hamstrings pull heavy with each step

    Once in a while,
    whenever it wants to,
    a large eagle can be found
    perched on beach wood
    He owns that beach and all who pass
    His royal brow gives no doubt

This is my favorite beach, you tell me, one foggy morning

We tried again to walk together
I walked 'til I reached the Eagle King,
you continued alone into the mist
Mystery always favored over familiar
I sit and watch you heavy step away

Alone you go into the fog
leaving me to sit with the eagle
You continue until a low cloud
consumes you from my sight

 I imagine you reach the end
 where the cliffs give way to the shore
 and the landscape bends around
 to the fields at Cattlepoint
 I saw you in my mind
 alone and happy with your thoughts
 and the sea

I sit and watch,
You walk and ponder

A year later,
You sat and watched
as I walked off the island
You let me go that year
just like I let you
walk the beach
alone

Island Winter

Fall is over
Frost is setting in
Clear sky or cloudy
Ice is found in the morning
Alone
Quiet
No birds
No visitors

The ocean is colder
The beach is empty
A gull stands watch
On a beach wood wall
Solitude
Peace
Breath seen
Waves heard

...it is winter

Rancid Blood

"Jesus asked him, saying, "What is your name?"
And he said, "Legion," because many demons had entered him."
    —Luke 8:30, Holy Bible, New King James Version

You sit across the table and smile
Eyes dark, glazed, fingers tap the table
As I search for words
What is your name?

A worm crawls inside
Eats the innards, of a rotten, soggy soul
You are dead, the you I knew
Died years ago
If only I could cast out demons
And send them into swine,
Alcohol no longer your blood
Sorry, but I have no words
The sight of you has stolen them
All I can do is hold your hand
I cannot climb your mountain
I cannot walk your path
I cannot fight your fight
This is a demon you must
Cast out of yourself
Every day

Homeless Person Less Than

I am a dirty demographic
The frog in the hand of a young boy
testing his powers

I am the lump of feather-bones
on a pine needle floor
poked at with a stick

> Mermaid with a black eye
> Blind Colossus walking in the street
> Hermes on a flat-tire bike

I am homeless
I will always be with you
I am broken never to be fixed

Lining of My Mind

Premonition stands outside the window,
framed to be seen,
stands politely 'til the door opens
the right door
at the right time
Future comes to me quickly
Tea or coffee?
A blanket for your lap?
It's cold outside where time weathers
as a Pacific swirls over the peninsula
      hooked on peaks
        cold. still.
It rains in my house.
The fire is out.
Wet paper see-throughs to wooden table.
Drips creep across the low areas, finds them all
—both the dark and the hidden.

I'm swept up in to this ungraspable moment
Future comes to visit.

What we desire more than seasons or weather
is the comfort of being a stranger,
more so with ourselves.
It is better not to know.

So I wait.

Wait for something that vanishes
as soon as it arrives.
Its appearance not unlike mowed lawn
—the stalk of the dandelion snapped.

It's there. We know it.
Whether we walk on it or not.
The merciless motor hums in the distance
and every so often
a breeze from the south carries the
leaky-green odor of grass

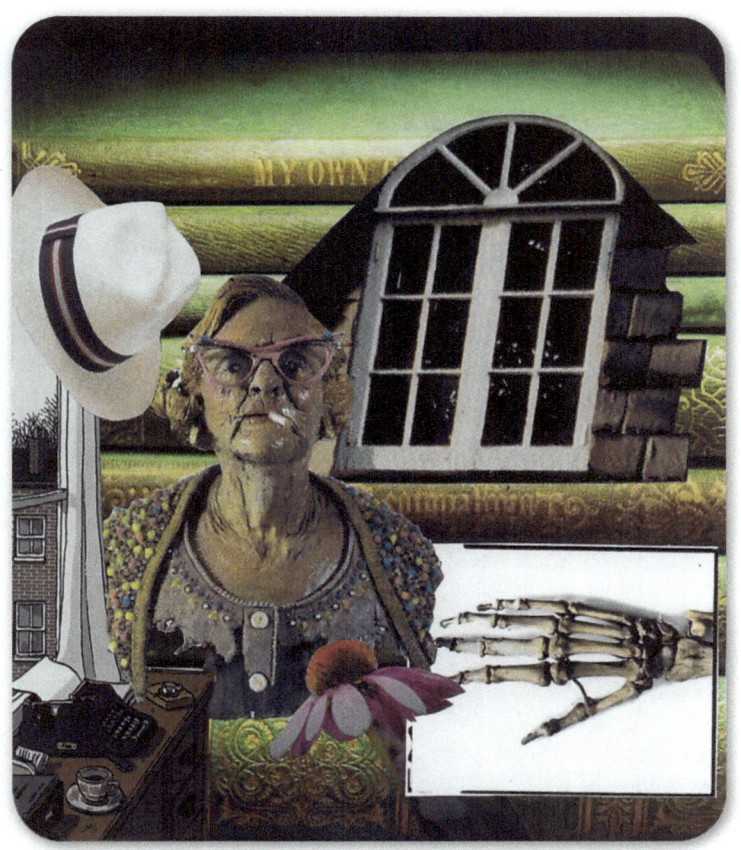

Four Minus Three

The sanctuary of four tulips
in a heavy glass jar
atop the round dining table
bathe in the afternoon sun

Church is found in
the smallest folded places
Between petals
Between panes

A god does not determine
who lives or dies
It is simply which seat you sat in at three a.m.
when a moose moves out from the brush

Three bleed out inside a crumpled ball of car

    while one

    if asked by any nurse or doctor

could tell you
what the family
ate for dinner
yesterday

Anything Else

It flakes off my shoulder when I bend down
Black trails my movement
Dark spots in the corner of my eye
let me know it's still there
A reminder of the charcoal thread
that ties me to my past
whisps of whispers from
that one night long ago

The hurt bleeds out
dribbles into a bucket
deeper than my lifetime will hold

Pain oozes
weeps down the bark of me
black like sap

Another God

I cannot sleep
next to you
The porch light
on the other side
of the curtains
tricks me awake

    You look frozen on a canvas,
    painted in oils by a master,
    shadows lightly brush your shape

I study the back of your head
your earlobe
a quiet beating vein
the hairline along the neck

There's a frame of freckles
below the shoulder blade
They look like Orion poised
with bow and arrow aimed upward

I am not your Merope taken by blind force
I am an Andromeda, wrists wrapped in iron
ready for monsters to decide loves fate

Gods visit the sheets of women
a vacation from eternity
Taste the finite in the kiss,
wipe their mouths with times mist

Tonight your constellation glows in porch light,
while I dream of everything I cannot have.

Tongue in Ink

The best poems are not written in ink but by the tongue
Spoken into the air never finding paper
Touched by the mist of breath against your neck
Said in the dark rooms where lovers meet

Not at all recorded nor syllables numbered
But art form just the same

Once activated and released the words are all lost
Left to moments that linger
Holding each other in a sweaty embrace
As if the sheets themselves are sentences

Introduction to Discovery

You are a question that must be answered

He touched me
He touched me
The way
I wanted him to
the way
I wished he would
He read my mind
and he touched me

His fingers moved along the ridges
of my galaxy in search of the ignition

>old crate of dynamite
>hidden in the shed
>sweats with glycerin
>delicate to movement
>so my love is for you

Drop that box! Start a bang!
Kick start a star to life

Use all fingers to read
me as a mystery novel
written in Braille
Every bump, knob and dip
a conjunction closer to knowing
the riddle of Eve

Groaning with Graffiti

"The poem unwritten, the act left in the mind, undone"
  —Denise Levertov

Three years the poem
of your body, of my
eyes upon your body
of my hands reading
each muscle—

> Stroking, sweeping the
> scent in the rite of
> worship, going down
> from the beat of a neck
> vein, along broad shoulders,
> twisted hair trail,
> belly to cock.

For three years that poem unwritten
trapped in my mind, not wanting to
share that I lie with Dionysus
fear that women would take my treasure,
or a god hearing my boast would end you

The Back of My Hand

It was that time of the
day when the light
gave away the distance
of each hill

The twilight swarm of gnats
and wishing cottonwood seeds
bounce off the windshield
in a rush to live and die

The dark sun wanting to set
took a rest over the last ridge

It was that place on the
highway where the lines
    solid yellow
     dotted white
    solid white
bend in unison to
show off its curves
like a lady in a corset

It was that time, that place
when you wiggled in your seat
turned a shoulder forward
looked at me and said
"I love you. You know I love you right?"

Your hand hugged mine
as we came to that point
in the pass where the
road is visible for miles

I saw it worming down around
ending with a sharp left
I knew—with no doubt
I knew it continued into
the Skagit Valley, pass the cafe
I knew we'd find the freeway
and reach our street by ten tonight

We'd both go to work in the morning
and the week would continue
into more weeks, months, and years...
and when you said you loved me
it was a lie

Morning Walk

This morning the clouds sleep
Ground fog rests silent in the hills
Clings to the Earth like a warm blanket
    Walk pass a van full of everything anyone owns,
    Even the owner. Slumped over, fast asleep,
    No blanket, two coats for insulation.

Dew still on the grass.
Crows and seagulls shout at each other.
Caws versus shrieks; calls of our hilltops
Wrestle with the sound of the sea.

Turning the corner, large black garbage bags
From the baseball stadium rip open;
Guts of popcorn and half eaten hot dogs spill out.
    Five seagulls look after it.
    With regal heads and crisp beaks.
    Soldiers, guarding a treasure.

On the next corner, a cherry tree shows off
Early fruit. Yellow, blending to orange,
By fall "cherry red" will be visually defined.

Next block over, I tiptoe by another man
Asleep in his car. Blue Ford Escort Wagon
is his address. Two in one morning.
A few evergreens over, a tent camp
lays beneath the heavy boughs.

Signs: For Rent. For Rent. For Rent.

I continue up towards the stadium,
Trek along a silent creek, full of water.
The surface so still you can dance on it.

Acknowledgments

I would like to gratefully acknowledge the journals, settings, and websites where these poems have been published or reviewed:

"No Marrow," *Clover, A Literary Rag*, Winter Edition 2012

"Ink Stained Hands," *Clover, A Literary Rag*, Winter Edition 2013

"The Lining of My Mind," *Clover, A Literary Rag*, Winter Edition 2015

"Death's Dip or Confession of a Mattress," *Clover, A Literary Rag*, Summer Edition 2016

"Rancid Blood," Bertolino, James. 2018. *Last Call - The Anthology of Beer, Wine & Spirits Poetry*. Tillamook, Oregon: World Enough Writers.

I would like to thank the Chuckanut Sandstone Writers and Bellingham Repertory Dance Company collaboration *Phrasings* chapbook (2011) and the anthology *Noisy Water, Poetry from Whatcom County, Washington*, Other Mind Press (2015) for publishing "Housekeeper" respectively.

I would like to thank *Levitate Literary Magazine* (2019) and *Cirque Journal* (2020) for publishing "Four Minus Three" respectively.

I am grateful to the Village Books Poetry Group, 2011-2016, which read the first versions of many of the poems collected here. Thank you for your voice and insight.

The poetry book *Tongue in Ink* is a collection of new and selected poems from the following publications by the author:

Laws, Shannon, *Madrona Grove: Poems written under the Canopy*, Bellingham, Washington. Chickadee Productions, 2012, second edition 2013.

Laws, Shannon, *Odd Little Things*. Bellingham, Washington: Chickadee Productions, 2014.

Laws, Shannon P. *Fallen: Poems*. Bellingham, Washington: Independent Writers' Studio Press, 2017.

Shannon Laws. *You Love Me, You Love Me Not*. MP3. recorded at Alpenglow Sound Studios, Bellingham, Washington: Chickadee Productions, 2019. Available at Bandcamp.com

https://www.youtube.com/@chickadeeproductions
https://www.instagram.com/shannon.chickadee/

About the Author

Shannon Laws is an award-winning poet, performer, and advocate for the arts. She has been recognized with two Mayor's Arts Awards and the Dr. Asha Bhargava Memorial Award — Community Champion. Her work has been featured in numerous journals and anthologies, and she has captivated audiences at esteemed literary events, including the Jack McCarthy Evergreen Invitational Slam, SpeakEasy, Poetry Night, Kitchen Sessions, and the West Coast Tagore Festival.

Beyond her writing and performances, Shannon actively fosters literary and artistic communities. Since 2022, she has curated *Corridor*, a monthly "found-art" zine project that showcases the work of more than 50 contributing poets and artists. She is also the founder and host of Poetry Club, an engaging discussion group established in 2015.

Shannon lives in Bellingham, Washington.

Learn more at shannonplawswriter.com

About the Artist

Kathleen A. McKeever lives on the edge of the Salish Sea. The collage illustrations she created for this book are made with scissors, cut paper, and glue.

www.ingramcontent.com/pod-product-compliance
Lightning Source LLC
Chambersburg PA
CBHW040848120626
46547CB00001B/73